Silas on Sundays

Story by Joel Shoemaker | Illustrations by Taranggana

WILDLING PRESS

Copyright © 2024 by Joel Shoemaker

All rights reserved. No part of this book may be reproduced, distributed, or transmitted in any form, by any electronic or mechanical means, without permission in writing from the publisher, except in the case of brief quotations published in articles and reviews and certain other non-commercial uses permitted by copyright law.

ISBN: 978-1-957833-13-2
LCCN: 2024934572

Designed by Michael Hardison
Edited by Christina Kann
Production managed by Mary-Peyton Crook
Proofread by Grace Ball

Printed in the United States of America

Published by

WILDLING PRESS

www.wildlingpress.com

For Nex

At home,
Silas can be
whoever they want.

On Monday,
Silas is the star quarterback.
They score a touchdown
and win the game every time!

On Tuesday,
Silas is the cheerleading captain.
G-O T-E-A-M!
They shout and pose from the very
tip tippy-top of the pyramid!

On Wednesday,
Silas is a famous actor.
They rehearse their lines
and act out their scenes
with pizzaz and gusto.
They even win an award!

On Thursday,
Silas is a ballerina.
They dance gracefully,
leaping and twirling about.
At the end of their show, the audience gives a
standing ovation and throws flowers up on stage.

On Friday,
Silas is a black belt in karate.
They karate-chop
their way through
six solid blocks of wood!

On Saturday,
Silas discovers a new star.
They perfect a peach pie.
They build houses.
They pilot an airplane.
They defend castles.

Saturdays are full of adventure!

For Silas,
Sundays are a
very different story.

On Sundays,
Silas's mother says,
"No, you can't wear that today."
Their father says,
"You have to sit still and listen, kiddo."

Monday Silas fights dragons,

and Tuesday Silas has a dance recital,

and Wednesday Silas is a classroom teacher,

and Thursday Silas is a doctor,

and Friday Silas does a spa day,

and Saturday Silas is
curious and confident
and thoughtful and goofy
and very, very brave.

Sunday, Silas pretends to be sick.
"I guess we can't go to church today."

On Monday and Tuesday,
Silas studies paleontology in library books.
On Wednesday and Thursday,
they find all of the fossils in their backyard.
On Friday,
they set up their fossil collection,
and on Saturday,
they show all their friends!

The next Sunday,
Silas **accidentally** oversleeps.
"I guess we missed church today," says Silas.

Monday Silas goes to the zoo,

and Tuesday they run a marathon,

and Wednesday they swim with dolphins,

and Thursday they paint their nails,

and Friday they lift weights,

and Saturday they go to the moon!

On Sunday,
Silas gets out of bed early
and makes a **HUGE** breakfast.
"I don't know what happened," says Silas.
"There's all this food. We have to eat it. I guess
we don't have time for church today."

Over breakfast, Silas says,
"I'm sorry we keep missing church."
Silas's parents realize something is amiss.
With a mouthful of pancakes,
Silas's father says, "Let's go to the park!"

Because the park has an elephant and a water fountain you can run through and a huge slide and many, many rocks, of course Silas agrees this is a very good idea indeed.

That Sunday,
Silas climbed on all the playground equipment and found all the cool rocks. And they also found a group of volunteers helping people in need.

"Excuse me," Silas says. "I'm sorry to tell you this, but you're standing on what might be a very valuable rock."

"Oh! Of course. I'm so sorry!" says the human as they step aside. "My name is Matt. I use he/him pronouns."

Silas looks up at him with curiosity. "Cool!" Silas picks up the rock, runs back to their parents, and brings them to the volunteers' table.

"This is Matt," Silas says to his parents. "He uses he/him. He has cross earrings and helps all kinds of people. He was kinda ruining this valuable rock with his feet, but I'm still pretty sure I want to go to his church."

"Next Sunday will be THE BEST!" Silas says.

And the following Sunday is the best.

On Sunday,
they go to the new church,
just like Silas suggested.

They are greeted by Matt and rainbows
and toyboxes and stuffed animals
and colors and rocking chairs
and music they can clap along to.
Almost on beat.

Here, Silas is loved. Everyone is.
Here, Silas is celebrated. Everyone is.
Here, Silas can sing, dance,
and wear what they choose,
and they can be precisely
who they want to be.

Silas loves Mondays.
They love Tuesdays
and Wednesdays
and Thursdays
and Fridays
and Saturdays.

Now, Silas loves Sundays too.

About the Author

JOEL SHOEMAKER has been a librarian for a decade and a magician for three! He lives in central Illinois with his husband, a frog, a fish, and his dog, Maximus. He consumes an inordinate amount of cheese.

Loved Silas on Sundays?

Check out these other works by Joel:

bacon grief
one of the only works of fiction for teens and tweens
to celebrate and affirm both faith and sexuality

Teeth & Crumpets: A Florilegium
a short story collection about teeth

About the Illustrator

LINTANG PANDU PRATIWI is a thirty-year-old illustrator and author from Indonesia. Through her art studio, Taranggana, she has illustrated more than one hundred picture books for various publishers and clients in the United States, Europe, and Asia. She loves art and nature, and is inspired by the ideas of nostalgic childhood innocence and the beautiful countryside.

Printed in the USA
CPSIA information can be obtained
at www.ICGtesting.com
LVHW071730110724
785237LV00003B/15

9 781957 833132